Postcards Home

Postcards Home

Dede Fox

INK
BRUSH
PRESS

ISBN: 978-0-9888632-5-5
Library of Congress Control Number: 2014947777

Manufactured in the United States

Ink Brush Press
Dallas

For Sara and Amy

Poetry from Ink Brush Press

Alan Birkelbach and Karla Morton, *No End of Vision: Texas as Seen by Two Laureates*
David Bowles, *Shattering and Bricolage*
Jerry Bradley, *The Importance of Elsewhere*
Millard Dunn, *Places We Could Never Find Alone*
Alan Gann, *Adventures of the Clumsy Juggler*
Jim McGarrah, *Breakfast at Denny's*
J. Pittman McGehee, *Growing Down*
Chris Ellery, *The Big Mosque of Mercy*
Charles Inge, *Brazos View*
Steven Schroeder, *a dim sum of the day before*
Steven Schroeder and Sou Vai Keng, *a guest giving way like ice melting*
Jan Seale, *Nape*
Jan Seale, *The Wonder Is*
W.K. Stratton. *Dreaming Sam Peckinpah*
Chuck Taylor, *At the Heart*
Jesse Waters, *Human Resources*
Scott Yarbrough, *A Sort of Adam Infant Dropped: True Myths*

For information on these and other Ink Brush Press books go to
www.inkbrushpress.com

Acknowledgments

I am grateful to the editors of the following journals and anthologies for publishing some of the poems that are now in this book.

Confessions of a Jewish Texan
di-verse-city
The Enigmatist
Houston Poetry Fest Anthology
Poetica
Poetry at Round Top
The Poetry Revolt
Sol
A Summer's Poems
Swirl
Texas Poetry Calendar

"Chapultepec Park" published by *di-verse-city*, 2008, won the Christina Sergeyevna Award.

Thank you to InPrint Houston and Dave Parsons for the 2006 Poetry Writing class that started me on this journey, to my critique buddies Ada, Arroz, Erica, Maryke, and John for helping me to up my game, to the MCLAC board for educating me, to John Milkereit for introducing me to Matt Riley who agented this book by posting my work on his blog, and to Jerry Craven for creating a beautiful cover and bringing this book to life. I appreciate all of you.

CONTENTS

I. Postcards

II. Fellow Travelers

III. Passages

I. Postcards

Chapultepec Park: September 25, 1968

Campsinos kneel like Diego Rivera's Flower Seller,
spread baskets of lilies, irises, sunflowers
fresh from the bud as the young woman
    who gathers them in brown arms,
    strolls through Chapultepec green,
    dreams of a lover among the helado vendors,
    peanut crunchers, pinwheel spinners, futbol players.
Overhead red and yellow balloons snare
        running children in their dangling strings.

    She follows a winding path to a sculpture garden
where sun-warmed statues embrace in a vacuum.
Like a shadow, silence fills the plaza. An absence of sound
pulls her from a flower-filled reverie.
        Her eyes widen.

    She catches her breath, darts through spiky bushes
to the broad Paseo de la Reforma, now still.
No rattling grimy cars, smoke-belching buses,
    shawl-draped women
        with bundles and babies.

Stiff-legged soldiers goosestep in tight rows,
rifles, bayonets, bazookas against their shoulders.
    At road's curve, tanks roll,
    mechanical monsters, geared,
    devour everything
        in their path. She runs.

Her sandals slap the tender undersides of bare feet
as she weaves in and out of razor straight lines,
blank-faced soldiers, blinded by command.

        Her heart
       pounds like their boots.

Pursued by Rivera's murals, Revolutions,
            memories, mothers' tales of uniformed rapes,
                            she tears across the avenue,
            trailing ripped lilies, bruised irises,
                                    crushed sunflowers.

For Diana la Cazadora

Your sharpened arrow pointed
north, once my compass,
directing me to all things unexplored,
waiting to be hunted
by someone eager and chaste.

Your sculpted body modeled
by a sixteen-year-old secretary
for Pemex, her payment
seeing her own form,
curved as the bow she held,
adorning La Reforma.

After the Decency League dressed
you in fabric underwear in 1942,
Juan Olaguibel, your creator,
hoping to later wrench them off,
girdled you in bronze
welded on only three points.

Like all those undressed
in the Sixties, you were damaged,
banished in 1970 to Ixmilquilpan,
a regent's native town, a new
virgin cast to take your place,
Sweet Guardian of Chapultepec.

Bureaucrats moved her too in 1974,
hid her in Ariel Park, for eighteen years.
Artists demanded her release,
her inaugural roundabout
the Paseo de la Reforma,
Walkway to Freedom.

Back home in 1992,
this violated virgin Diana
la Cazadora, naked, bow drawn
with one perfect arrow,
still points to shooting stars,
hunts beasts from the North.

Cutting Lemons with Pete Seeger: 1970

Tuning his guitar in the kitchen,
he smiled, talked to the college girl
who sliced the lemons in precise pieces,
first the length, then each half into six
perfect wedges. She blushed, ignored
juice stinging her chapped, cracked hands.

Her supervisor, a middle-aged woman
from The Hill, charged into the kitchen,
shooed him out with her snapping dish towel,
sent the girl into the coffee house to collect
white cups, stained with coffee, saucers
soiled with cigarette ashes.

She entered the smoky fog of a bearded
would-be-philosopher, too lost in thought
about how the proletariat should revolt
to accommodate her and a cart of dirty dishes.
Climbing over his legs, she emptied his ashtray,
eyed his chambray work shirt with irritation.

Her shift ended as she listened to the dishwasher's
percussion, its thumps fused with Seeger's music.
"Mama don't allow no guitar playing here."
But scholarship students have to study.
Books tucked under one arm, she walked
past Seeger in the lobby, his rehearsal in exile.

He nodded and smiled. Even banished
by the kitchen tyrant, Pete Seeger knew his audience.

Prisms

At a graying frame house
we climb creaking steps,
listen for the porch boards' welcome,
knock on side-by-side screen doors,
sniff the fan-generated breeze
that always smells vaguely of cabbage,
and wait for white-haired Mrs. Goff,
the seamstress, to welcome us.

Once inside, Mother, a suit draped
over one arm, warns me to sit
quietly in a chair next to a lamp
hung with glass prisms that capture
hazy light drifting through a long
row of open windows.

I imagine a lonely princess
wearing those dangling crystals
strung into a jeweled necklace.
She's trapped in a tall tower
where rainbows flicker
across patterned wallpaper.

Soft voices drift from the next room.
Mother and Mrs. Goff pull straight
pins from an apple pin cushion,
huddle over Daddy's jacket, now spread
across a groaning ironing board.
As transparent as those prisms,
I disappear, refracting
light into spectral colors.

Schnucks Paradise Market: 1971

A Garden of Eden day
too pretty to ride to the grocery store
in a boyfriend's beige Bug.
She leaves her bra dangling
from a doorknob and throws on
a loose, gauzy green dress.
Pausing on the steps, she inhales
the scent of roses
and her newfound freedom.

Later, browsing through the fruit bins
at Schnucks Market, she admires
the Artist's palette, selecting
a banana, green grapes, and a flawless
apple. A serpent appears
as she moves to the bread
section, searching for a hearty Jewish
rye among the rows of white bread.

He slithers up to her.
"I'm a photographer," he says.
"Would you model for me?"
She raises her eyebrows.
Curly-haired, brown-eyed girls
with un-Twiggy-like curves
rarely grace pages of magazines.

Ignoring the matrons at their flanks,
he presses on. "I pay well."
And he mentions a sum unfamiliar
to someone who busses tables
and cuts lemons at a college coffee house.
Reaching for a firm, thick loaf,
she murmurs, "What kind of pictures?"

He stumbles over his answer.
"Tasteful ones, of course."

Perhaps he thinks her a Fontbonne girl,
one untrained in the art of questioning,
but she attends the other college
and inquires, "With or without clothes?"
He draws back his head
and hisses, "I saw you bouncing
down the street, so free and easy."
The bread's cellophane wrapper
crackles in her tightening fist.

At home, the un-bagged groceries warm
on the counter as she reaches for her bra.
Biting into a freshly washed
apple, she sighs.
Restraint has never felt so liberating.

Alluvium

Under scuttle gray clouds, in flashes
of moonlight, she sees waves
splash over yellow headlights,
water rush beneath her car door.
It licks her sandaled toes.

                            She raises her feet,
checks the backseat, where in pours a rising tide.
With sweaty hands, she tugs on slippery handles,
uses both feet to fight the surge,
pushes open a leaden door.

At last she touches ground,
wades into the roadbed. Shrouded
in white, she peels back her tangled wet dress,
frees her legs, and thrashes through current.
Murky waters pull at her thighs.
      She struggles to higher ground,
                      away from the bayou's dark arms,
                              bloated rats, swimming snakes.

The young woman scales the bank, slides
in mud, clings at last to a wooden post. Shivering,
she pulls herself along, winces as rusty barbs
rake her hands, the fence her guide wire.

An hour later, a tow truck driver stops on a steaming road,
discovers her abandoned car, headlights dimming.
Keys dangle from a drowned ignition.
On the floorboard a western mosquito fish
                          floats belly up in pooled water.

Enchanted

A foggy dawn in the woods
gauzy patches of white filigree
line trails, torn pieces
from a wedding veil
of a heartbroken princess,

Or wisps of smoke
from the fiery dragon
 that stole her prince.

Perhaps forest fairies forgot
to hide hammocks, hung
in tiers from winding vines.

With Arachne's artistry,
spiders spin nets, trap
birdsongs in silvered threads
beaded with Eos' tears,
soon dried by Apollo.

The Uninvited Guest

Every year he appeared at our Seder,
lurked in my grandfather's slight shadow,
brandished a shank bone at Hebrew chants,
gorged at our Passover feast. When he tasted
our bitter herbs, beet-red horseradish, we turned
away, frightened by his stained lips, crimson
as flames that curled Haggadah pages, burned
shtetyls to ashes, scattered by angry winds.
With his every bite, matzo cracked like rifle shots,
or wooden stakes splintering skulls. His eyes
scorched us as we ate eggs, salted by tears.
Opening the front door for the prophet Elijah,
we shivered, saw shadows dance through the night
like drunken Cossacks waving bloody sabers.

When my grandfather died, the uninvited never returned.
Today bridal wreath and azaleas bloom along our brick
walls. With one of four cups, we toast our grandfather
for oceans crossed, new ways learned, traditions upheld.
But opening the door for Elijah, we shiver, watch
and wonder when and where the uninvited will appear
again, this shape-changer. We pray for all in bondage,
and say once more, "Next year in Jerusalem."

On the Trail

Even Chihuly couldn't master this:
crystal leaves, delicate,
translucent, backlit by dawn.

Branches strike poses,
dabs of watercolor green
on their fingertips.

Tiny yellow and white petals
drift through the air,
an offering, communion.

Squirrels, trapeze artists,
cross midair, descend trees
downed by winter storms.

A blue jay flaps, chitters,
chases a gray tail up a steep roof,
far from nestlings concealed below.

Songs fill the air,
repetitive trills, cricket calls
secret rustlings in the brush.

Beyond the green veil, cars
whoosh, trailers rattle, trucks grind,
drivers miss spring.

Summer Song

Pumping legs propelled
our bicycles to Evergreen Park pool.
Heated up by July's fire
we'd zip under the cold outdoor
shower, getting just wet enough
to avoid those whistle-blowing lifeguards.

Fearless Adri cannon-balled
into the deep end, while I'd watch,
clinging to aquamarine tiles lining the sides
and Viv, hand resting on the silver rails,
awaited an applauding audience as
she descended steps in the shallow end.

But we always met underwater, our ritual
the pretend tea parties at the bottom,
bubbles surfacing with our laughter.
We twisted, hair streaming behind us,
made silly faces, pretended to be
improperly proper ladies.

Sometimes we'd risk hide-and-seek
with pennies needed for snow cones--
orange, strawberry pink, and my favorite
lime. After a swim we flopped down
to crunch ice, sip syrup, wave to friends.
Spiky weeds tickled our damp legs.

Sticky, sun-warmed, sleepy,
we'd mount rattling bikes,
plastic streamers flying
from handles and spindly spokes
as we raced each other home,
last one there a rotten egg.

Haiku Variations on a Maple

I.
Like an Escher print,
green wallpaper leaves transform,
flutter like white moths.

II.
Shimmying woman
in a silver sequined dress
dances to wind's song.

Bible Belt

Along abandoned streets, grass scorches
brown, brittle as pine needles. Dusty
trees drop faded leaves on empty
parks, stilled swings, vacant
lawn chairs. Smoke rises
from deserted oil drums.
Phantoms barbecue,
too hot to cook in kitchens.

Under white skies,
heat waves from glaring highways,
rises through floorboards,
burns soles of booted feet. Unseen
drivers, behind blinding
reflections, darkened windows
and sunglasses, still squint.

Blistering sun peels skin, paint,
steams radiators, stalls trucks
along dusty roads. Stranded
riders swig bottled water,
hot enough to make tea.
Everyone prays for salvation.

Cold Comfort

We cross the threshold, shove
each other through gas fumes
from the leaky stove, rush to be first
to pull down the cool metal handle.

I capture the treasure on the tray
wedged between refrigerator and freezer
where Grandma stores a ribbed bottle of Coke.
iced to perfection, a rare treat we must share.

We fight over the opener too.
I snap off the metal cap;
its serrated edges nip fingertips.

As I anticipate arguments over dividing lines,
who gets to drink first
whether foam is fizz or spit,

I grab a jelly jar from the tiled counter,
pour in my portions to savor alone,
drown your complaints in carbonated bubbles.

Icy slivers slide over my tongue
As I savor the syrupy sweetness,
Drain the cup before you can ask for more.

Empty, the chipped glass rim warns
of swallowed shards, sharpened
fragments of our enmity and love.

Dreamsicles

Two tiny cowboys straddle bikes
where the path ends at a busy road,
holler louder than canned music from the ice cream truck.
    "We can't cross the street!
     We can't cross the street!"
They call to the boy on the other side,
who roams free from parental restrictions.
    "Take my wallet.
     Tell him we have money."

Faint music lures away the wild one.
    "No. I'll tell him you're here."
Frenzied pumping ensues, while the stuck ones wail,
    "We can't cross the street!
     We can't cross the street!"
Their pain fills trail walkers with angst,
reminds all of the ones that got away-
ice cream cones that toppled, balloons that escaped,
a first love, perfect job, novel almost published.

We stand among the sunlit pines, fight
grief when the music stops, hold our breaths
until it starts up again,
         grows louder,
             closer.
The tinny tune expands to a sonata,
    notes soaring in the summer sunset.

Clover Park

Boys climb playground equipment,
hide behind trees, under picnic tables,
shoot stinging pellets from air rifles,
argue about who's out, who's dead.
Shouts punctuate actions;
their voices set the rhythm
for adults walking through the woods.

In June a crowd gathers,
memorializes a soldier,
celebrates his twentieth birthday,
talks about a boy who played war here.

Neighbors listen as humble ministers,
proud politicians stand on gazebo steps,
protected from the sun and other hazards,
speak of the young man who loved God,
shot guns on command.
Boy Scouts raised slack flags.

Now his mother lies on dedicated
benches under night's camouflage,
seeks comfort from stars,
asks why her son.

Fourth of July in Clover Park:
Boys shoot firecrackers,
their whistles, bangs, smoky
detonations behind her house.
Stop!

5546

I have worn your street number
like a hated tattoo--
removal will be painful.

Inspectors say your cast iron pipes decayed
under a slab riddled with fault lines,
like our grieving family.

Nine months to repair,
nine months to say
good-bye.

Notes flutter from every open drawer;
reminders of things lost and found,
found and lost.

What treasure lies beneath layers of labels
peeled from the phone? A number
to reconnect a mother's scattered thoughts?

At the bottom of a painted wooden bowl
lie memories of a father's fingers cracking
pecans with a nutcracker, silver as tears.

In bedrooms
no sock left unknotted,
no pocket unchecked.

Many spill hidden riches:
an old letter, a tarnished spoon,
watches repaired by Grandpa's steady hands.

Bright patches inside faded wallpaper
trace spaces once filled with grandchildren's art;
stair-stepped little ones once pointed with pride.

Will buyers know there are mismatched door keys
four, the number of children raised here,
each unique?

5546, a street number,
imprinted memories,
echo of heartbeats.

Green Glass Bowl

Blown surface ripples like flesh,
its air pockets trap breaths,
exhalations of the artist.

For years it cups
pounds of ripening tomatoes
bananas, apples, peaches.

With one jolt or spin
it could shatter, but our final
purchase survives us.

The Wailing Wall: 2000

Fed by murmured prayers
feathery tufts of hendane
and snapdragons
cascade from Jerusalem limestone
like hanging baskets
from the Tower of Babylon.

Hebrew chants harmonize
with haunting wails,
the Muslim call to prayer.
Tzitzis dance from tallitot of joyful men
holding high the Torah,
scrolls open to reveal the Eternal Word.

Fingertips linger
on sun-warmed rocks.
press paper into tiny crevices.
I close my eyes and listen.
Captured dreams and prayers whisper (forever),
mingle with tears for unrealized peace.

Snapshots: Road to the Kinneret

I.
From Mt. Gilboa's veins
warm waters pool at Gan Haslosha,
bubble up around flat rocks,
stepping stones across millenia,
wash away scorched dust,
predatory footprints,
truncated cries of the vanquished,
dried blood from Masada.

II.
Beneath hanging gardens,
green-leafed screens,
Muslim women in white hijaabs,
leaden black abayas
sit in stony crevices.
whisper in tepid shadows,
listen to the rush, water over rock,
while brief-clad sons splash,
cool in a Garden of Eden.

III.
Stones,
sharp as spears,
infinite as tears,
sanded by wind without end,
or weighted as burdens
carried by nomads,
scatter across Rachel's grave
remembrances for Israel's poet
placed by a hundred hands.

Emily Dickinson at the Corner Pub

I've grown more like Emily than I'd like to admit.
My cloistered life confuses my children.
I sit at my writing desk for hours,
stare out the window at vagrant cats
who sniff and pad through yaupon and azaleas,
search for shadowy napping spots,
plot nocturnal attacks. Trees frame my view,
dropping prickly sweet gum balls, sunset leaves.

In December I venture out, drive through the night,
to deliver Emily's birthday cake to the Corner Pub.
Unmarked road changes confuse me,
or maybe I'm reconsidering a word in a poem.
I ram my careful Camry onto a curb, and clatter
down Main Street, the engine in its death throes.

Still I carry in Emily's white frosted delight,
wonder what she'd think about this crowd,
spouting her lines and their own,
between rounds of Shiner Bock.
Like me, she might sit near the door,
lick icing from a sticky fork, listen
to her fellow poets, wait for the AAA
wrecker, an early exit, and a ride home.

Within a week, however, a moon-roofed
Accord with a black-leather interior and XM
radio roars my name from a back alley.
I ditch the weary gray sedan and Emily
to speed away with Billy Collins.

Taunted

Angry gusts stripped tree bark,
shredded muscles of open-armed
oaks, once strong enough for children
to climb, once green enough to shelter
all beneath broad leaves. Now piled
high, brittle branches crackle,
"You can't."

Wedged in the V between curb and
driveway, limbs, twisted and torn,
hide their scars in a bed of debris.
Leaves contract, crumble with the passing
of day after sunny day while pine needles
leech color, fade like brown dye on gray hair,
whisper in the wind,
"You can't."

Too late, after the raking, the shoveling,
the stacking, the help from others,
officials bark orders to sort out plastic bags,
their slick surfaces buried in the swollen
heap, a silent reproof. FEMA trucks
with impossibly tall sides growl past
this unruly mound, mock me.
"You can't move us.
What downed you?"

Out of Darkness

A bus rattles up the mountain,
rumbles around a curve. Darkness
obscures what lies ahead. Brakes squeal.
Doors thump open.

Silent pilgrims file out,
feel their way, hands grasping metal rails,
cold as obsidian. A colored canvas
washed in black ink lies below the horizon.

They wait, witness increasing incandescence,
ethereal like a UFO. When ghostly shapes
emerge from ultramarine blues, observers
stir along the rail, pull cameras from bags.

Metallic clicks and murmurs rise like chants, prayers.
In the distance, curved white, a river etches its way,
carves rock into sculptures of unnatural grace. Petrified
strata glow, change colors, as sun ascends from stone,
welcomes all to daily revelation,
sunrise at the Grand Canyon.

Recreation

A beloved deck,
surrounded by Sago palms
Red Yucca, Indian Hawthorne,
its bench the perfect place
to pose family pictures,
pot plants, rest and read

First came the bird droppings,
squirrel gnawed railings,
splintered acorn shells.
Then came the plagues:
wood rats, carpenter ants,
skunks, snakes, dead possums

Time to set aside the bench
rip up the boards
one by one
expose those things
that thrive in darkness,
feed on remains

Dry them up,
rake them out,
level the loam,
lay down flagstones
flush with the earth
strong in the sun

Postcards Home

In the first photo your cheek presses against a friend's.
Behind your aviator's shades, your eyes shine as you fly
in a biplane high above the Florida Keys, a first adult adventure.
Through the years, you have sent postcards from China,
Japan, Taiwan. There you are under a banana leaf
in a Costa Rican rainforest, in the lap of a bearded man
at a Puerto Rican baseball game, dancing in Buenos Aires,
feasting on beef in Argentina. And those literary experiences--
reading poetry by the light of a Scottish sunrise, reciting
Shakespeare at the Globe Theatre, sipping wine and discussing
Wilde at Oxford, not to mention that cruise of the mythical Greek islands.
Of course you pose with the David in Italy. Digital clicks capture
moments you sky dive, then snorkel at the Great Barrier Reef,
hike in New Zealand, bike down the side of a Hawaiian volcano.
So many journeys to places I, your mother, may never see.
But in that last photo, an ultrasound, black and white waves
rock a new life. A tiny creature, heart fluttering, floats in its own sea.
Mouth open, it searches for a microscopic thumb. I know
none of your travels compare to the odyssey just begun.

A Piece of the Rock

Bells at St. Vincent de Paul
ring in 9:00 o'clock mass
as spectators carrying lattes
parade down Holcombe,
eager to witness the implosion,
another piece of my childhood reduced
to limestone and red granite shards.

Detonations destroy the Prudential
building in seventeen seconds,
erased like the Shamrock,
where only the parking garage remains,
feeding an insatiable need for fees.

Every week, on our way to pray,
my father drove past the fountain
in front of the Prudential,
where a recumbent man and woman
rose in stone from the "Wave of Life,"
naked as Adam and Eve.

They faced each other,
the man's hand resting on the woman's foot,
a child between them,
held aloft by strong arms.
In their serene pool seven shells sprayed
peace far more powerful than any prayer.

Fireworks

On the hill we watch
reflections of their sparks
ripple across the lake.

Below us on the shore
little Charlotte sits
on her father's shoulders,
calls the colors: purple
yellow, orange
red, white, and blue!

After the final percussion,
rumbles fade to silence.
Invisible boats stream north,
starboard lights, green-eyed
rusalki, glide through the night.

"I'm afraid," my daughter says,
her voice a whisper in the dark.
"I know," I answer,
imagining her open hands
resting on her blossoming belly.

Arrivals

Bruised burgundy
twin aliens lie,
chests fluttering,
behind layers of Plexiglas.
Loose skin dangles
from diminutive limbs
devoid of fat.

Laden with umbilical tubes
gold heart-shaped monitors,
machines blowing air
through stretched nostrils,
they fight for survival
on an unfamiliar planet.

Masked scientists
play Jacob's ladder,
weave sterile hoses
in intricate designs.
Gloved hands unravel
fragile connections,
hopes, prayers, knotted
neonatal dreams.

Glow

Out of blue shadowed woods, fireflies
dart through leafy hedges,
drift up in silence, swimming
to the moon in shimmering chains.
A round-shouldered man watches
from a screened porch
       as he rocks a restless baby.

In a world too hot and dry for magic,
he hasn't seen them for years,
thought they no longer existed.
Now he knows he can chase them,
chase them with his grandbaby
       beneath a summer moon.

He descends weatherworn
steps, captures one, feels it flutter
in his closed hand. His round-eyed
grandson solemnly studies the spaces
between his trembling fingers
       and sees it glow.

Shrinky Dinks

Sisters perch on a shared bar stool,
their smiles illuminated by light
from the oven window.
Plastic disks, rainbow colored,
curl, then flatten on aluminum foil.

The girls jump down, cheer,
point, and climb up again.
Seconds drag as they watch
Grandma remove them,
wait for them to cool.
At last they are ready.

Grandma smiles at them
but wonders which shrank more,
the plastic or her integrity
when she bought crafts
from a store that refuses
to carry Chanukah decorations.

March Memory

Cool concrete sweats under
open palms and fingertips.

She huddles on the porch, knees up
legs bent, close to her body,

a small animal, safe
and warm in a cozy lair.

Bamboo shades bang
against wooden beams.

Leaning against the cedar shakes,
she listens for the rain's heartbeat.

Gusts of wind drive a fine
mist through the screens,

with scents of wet earth,
spring's promise.

Here and Now

When happiness comes my way
I savor every drop,
swirling it in a crystal goblet,
sniffing its fragrance
before drinking deeply.
I lick my lips,
not wanting
to lose
any
of its
sweetness,
clinging to
its memory
as long
as
I
can.

Poetry

Wrapped in cellophane,
Some poems are understood
In a single glance.

Others offer glimpses of meaning,
As if seen through diaphanous layers,
A soaring ballerina's skirt.

At times readers crack geodes.
Rough surfaces disguise jeweled interiors,
Light captured in crystals.
Others remain impenetrable.

Readers,
Writers
Long for that
    gift of clarity,
    moment of grace,
    perfect gem,
    millisecond of connection,
    antidote to pain.

II. Fellow Travelers

Bewitched

No evil fairy heaped curses upon
this charmed child with hair like swirled
honey, chocolate brown eyes, creamy
skin sweet with kisses. Laughter bubbled
from her, sweet grandchild, long awaited.

Grandmother, overjoyed, wove
dresses from the finest flax, combed
wool for the softest blankets, knit
tiny sweaters until her fingers bled.
Gnarled walking cane in hand, she hobbled
long miles, presented her gifts to the royal family.

Ladies-in-Waiting recoiled at the pungent
odor of the salve spread on Grandmother's aching
limbs, covered their noses with lace handkerchiefs
while children hid behind their skirts, pointed and
jeered at Grandmother's simple clothes and manners.
Blushing, her princess daughter turned away,
distracted the court with the antics of her baby.

Grandmother limped home. Soon twisted
vines tightened over her cottage, so far from the palace.
The old woman no longer threw open shutters, lost
hope of seeing her daughter or granddaughter travel
down the slow path in her dark woods.

The curse was on her, Grandmother gifted
with a precious child she could neither see nor hear
nor smell nor hold close.

Anger fueled Grandmother's stone oven,
with a fire so intense that it baked her into a wrinkled
old crone who hacked away entanglements.

She covered her cottage with sweets--
honey swirls, chocolate kisses, creamy caramels--
waited to lure small strangers inside, ones so delicious
that she could keep them caged, fatten them,
                              and eat them up.

Barricades

Fence posts, like six-foot guards,
stand at attention around three sides
of their house, not even a single knothole
hints at what lies beyond.

On the trail, I creep past their backyard
in winter when fence boards contract
leaving small gaps, an invitation
to peek as I walk.

Like the biting wind, disbelief
nips at me as I see a screen on their patio,
perhaps a massive bed sheet pulled
tight over PVC pipes to block all view.

What fears, taut as that sheet
must haunt those uneasy neighbors
who prefer viewing a blank screen
when on the other side
through a winter wood
cardinals fly.

Reading the Shelves

Librarians read shelves by placing books in order,
Alphabetically and numerically:
NIE for Nietzsche follows NAD for Nader
As surely as 032 Guinness Book of World Records
Precedes 292 Greek Myths.
796.7 Monster Trucks roar past 629.8 Robots
And 796.334 Soccer scores
Against the 796.323 Chicago Bulls.

Librarians pull books forward on the shelves,
Volumes shoved roughly against inflexible shelving,
Release pressure from delicate spines,
Coax book supports into place,
Shelf by shelf, row by row, day after day,
Bring order to chaos
And enlightenment to the masses.

At home books stack up or slip away.
Tattered self-help books spill over into open places
Where Virginia Woolf once lived in perfect harmony with Heinlein,
Dave Barry, and the Reader's Digest Home Repair Book.
Dust bunnies hide behind Goodnight Moon,
And Shel Silverstein searches for The Missing Piece.

Once a year librarians snake around public libraries in Conga lines
While book companies feed them chocolates.
No wonder bartenders count out cases and pat their pockets
When the library convention comes to town.

Adath Emeth: "Children of Truth"

I found them in the barrio,
my great-grandparents from Valkowisk,
unexpected their location near the Fiesta
Motel and Bolillo Bakery.

At Adath Emeth Cemetery they are buried
in concrete-lined crypts, covered with gravel,
fired white in the Texas sun. Summer
green lawns vibrate from the nearby highways' hum.

I place stones on their graves, wonder if
their spirits wander next door to Canino's
Farmer's Market, where they can sample plump
bananas, juicy mangoes, and ripe melons,

forbidden fruit no more,
these gifts from the Almighty
by way of McAllen, Brownsville, Monterrey,
or maybe they feast on flautas at Tampico's.

Fiddling Klezmorim drift from graves,
join the merry Mariachis.
Tonight Mendel and Esther dance,
old bones rattling in time.

For the Exterminators

after Edward Hirsch's "For the Sleepwalkers"

Tonight I want to say something in recognition
of exterminators, those un-lauded heroes, skilled
eradicators of vermin that creep unseen

behind our spackled walls, thump around
attic haunts, wallow in shower drains clogged
with sloughed skin, soap-scummed hair.

Masters of the extinguishing arts
dispense poisons, provide protection
from pests, real and imagined.

They direct venomous sprays,
while we, the sanctimonious, flee,
returning only when the fumes are gone.

Their hands protect our illusions.
our insistence that our needs,
our desires supersede theirs.

Rotten

Ah, Lucy,
you are such a bitch.
Men open doors for you
without your offering
a word of thanks.
You toss your head
as they escort you
under arched branches
along winding paths
strewn with wildflowers.

Nothing common for you.
Ignoring those who serve,
you dine on golden
delicious apples and duck.
Your carefully coiffed hair
requires visits to the salon
where you sit to one side
and gaze out the window,
far too superior to interact
with other bitches.

I'd tell you the truth
about your shameful behavior,
but you'd simply turn away,
brown eyes averted
nose raised in haughty
distaste at harsh words,
loud recriminations.
Sometimes I wonder
if either of us realizes
you are only a dog.

Waiting

Eggshell clouds hang low,
promise snow,
Lone boy perches
on a stone wall
under a hickory tree
and waits,

watches squirrels crisscross
bare branches,
listens to birds, wings
flapping, call.
Something's coming
soon, soon.

Muted skies fill with night.
Streetlights kindle.
Headlights streak yellow
across empty lawns.
Silence comes,
deepens.

A woman emerges
from porch shadows,
takes his cold hand in hers,
leads him inside.
No one's coming,
not tonight, not tonight.

Symphony Salon Series

Medicine patch behind one ear,
he snorts, hacks, spits
into a handkerchief,
and mouths to his wife,
"I'm not doing very well."
She turns her back, waves
away hot flashes with a program,

and leans far into the aisle,
mesmerized by the pianist
Jon Kimura Parker. His fingers,
hummingbird's wings, fly
up and down the keys, music
moving in ways words cannot.

Under a spotlight, Parker's wife
Aloysia Friedman embraces
her viola. Her bow vibrates
strings of souls, her anesthesia
Morpheus. In the audience
eyes lose focus, shoulders drop.

Next Schubert's "Wanderer"
Fantasie Opus 15, a seduction,
invites the audience inside,
builds note by billowing
note to a crescendo,
until there is nothing else.

In the silence that follows, fingers
uncurl, tense lines ease around lips.
No longer coughing, the gray-
haired listener locks eyes
with his wife and smiles.
She places a hand on his thigh.

Devil's Dance

inspired by *The Slave Dancer* by Paula Fox

They kidnapped him, fatherless
boy, from the New Orleans docks,
held him captive in a slave ship.
Stench from the hold, from past
voyages, overwhelmed him as he fought
for survival among savage sailors,
mercenaries, traders in human flesh.

At Whydah in the Bight of Benin,
they filled the hold with chained
natives, ordered the boy to play
his fife on deck, where they brought
half-dead Africans to dance, forced
exercise to reduce financial losses
along the hellish Middle Passage.

Like musicians at Auschwitz,
commanded to play Wagner,
the enslaved were tortured by brutes
who demanded that they dance
to their own execution marches.

The survivors, a boy with a fife,
men with scarred ankles,
women with tattooed arms,
never again piped another note,
raised leaden feet or bow to string,
each note a dagger.

Chasing Tails

For fifty years
you've followed her,
a panting puppy
longing for an approving pat.
Your sad brown eyes never see
there's only room in her mirror
for self-reflection.

Phyllis

held her neuroses
closer than her children,
existed in the center of
her self-created cosmos.

Between (the lines)

tangled layers:
frosty nouns
racing verbs
adjusted adjectives
limp adverbs
split infinitives
dancing participles
metaphorical memories
sticky similes
whispered hyperbole
wet onomatopoeia
feral personification
twisted syntax
what matters most
unsaid

Solitaire

She sits in the middle of the bed,
one leg bent at the knee,
foot tucked under. Her legs
form a number four
like the cards she flips and scans
with the intensity of a surgeon
deciding where to make the next cut.

She doesn't lift her head
when he approaches.
She doesn't move to one side
to make room for him.
So he slides around her, lies on his side.
His body bends at an awkward angle,
outside her perimeter and her game.

Thick black hair curtains
her face as she leans over the cards.
He longs to pull it back, to feel
its silky length between his fingers,
each strand one of so many barriers
between them.

Deferential

Damn them to Dante's Eighth Circle,
those polite drivers with the right of way
who slow on approach to the intersection
where you wait and wait and wait
at the stop sign for them to go.

There's the man who holds the door for you,
then waves for you to hurry up,
His face reddens with each
of your labored steps, weighed
down with a toddler and diaper bag,

And the hostess who smiles and bows
while escorting you to the table
closest to the clanging kitchen
or the foul bathroom
or the crying baby.

Protect me from agreeable co-workers
who acquiesce to every suggestion
only to stage eruptions worthy of Mt. Vesuvius
when expected to follow through
 on anything.

Or the obsequious child
who whispers incitements
to a volatile sibling
destined to detonate
within reach of an impatient adult.

My favorite, the grinning, nodding mate
who looks right at you while wondering
what time would be best to meet
his girlfriend at the Comfort Inn.
Damn them all.

Hungry

She was locked in, longing
for a bone that I, distracted,
tossed, a treat that rolled
outside the crate.

She angled a paw between
black bars, a failed attempt to get
what was just beyond her reach.
Her tongue unfolded, licking cold
metal but never quite touching bone.

No one was there to hear her whining
as the sun's rays poured into the room,
bleached the tile floor white, heated
the savory marrow while she paced
her cage, sniffing the meaty aroma.

As light dimmed, grew denser, exhausted
by longing, she dropped into sleep,
dreamed of tasting the saliva-softened rib,
awakened in darkness to a dry throat,
lapped a little water from a gnawed bowl.

When, at last, I turned the key in the lock,
our dog, after all those hours, looked up
at me, wagged her tail, licked my hand
before she retrieved the bone. She loves
me, even if you cannot.

Sweet Tooth

Always the charmer, he brings
three cupcakes for their dimpled
daughter's twenty-seventh birthday,
invites his ex-wife to join them,
inquires about her family,
refers to a book on faith,
while she places her cupcake
in the freezer because it's Passover.
Maybe he remembers or maybe
this is his fiction, an amicable divorce.

But Red Riding Hood
knows her wolf. She will remove
the cupcake, frozen like their almond
eyed daughter, who has shunned
men since her father, howling,
went on the prowl. Red will pack this
icy cupcake in her brittle basket,
give it chilled to Grandma,
who has lost her memory,
but found her sweet tooth.

Corralled

She sees them flow over the ridge,
a wave, manes flying, tails splashing
high, backlit by a lingering sunset.
Her breath catches as they swim
down the hill. Sinuous brown bodies twist,
liquid legs lift and touch and lift again,
They stream across the meadow
toward the corral.

Loose hair swinging, the woman enters
the barn, passes the pen of a pacing stallion,
crosses to a stall where she lifts her foot,
rests it on a splintered rail, watches a blacksmith
remove a shoe from a mare who kicks him.
He kicks back, warns her mares often mate
with bared teeth, can cripple a male.
She smirks, reminds him stallions bite
necks, sometimes draw blood.

Harvest

She tugs at husks, so tight!
peels them back over her hand
so they form wheat-colored petals,
turns her bouquet clockwise,
labors over drying strips,
hopes she'll find even rows,
sweet kernels.

She tugs at husks, so tight!
longs for silk to soften
work-worn fingers,
cling to threadbare jeans,
fears she'll find blackened
teeth, gaps, mold, blight,
a barren cob.

Flame

You sucked up all the oxygen,
left me gasping, but still I loved you.
At times you radiated light,
brightened my darkest corners.
I held my hands to your fire,
and smiled even when your smoky
glances left others weak-kneed and panting.

But when your heart burned blue,
I backed away from your searing
intensity, cowered as you ravaged
everything in your path.
I prayed for your fury to subside,
held my breath until, ragged, it fueled
more sparks, re-ignited firestorms.

Now I hide in dark recesses, weep
holes, or insulated air pockets,
never whispering the unspeakable;
I want you to die
before you destroy
our smoldering house,
before I am only embers and ashes.

Feed the Hungry

artists offer bowls for sale
swirling plums on a glazed black surface
waves of ocher and olive washing a sandy center
scarlet Chinese letters supine on an ivory bed
a maze of gray lines, crackled by flames
stripes of teal and rust
lips kissed with vermillion
empty bowls

milling shoppers seek perfect matches
round or fluted, glossy or muted
symmetrical or irregular
narrow-based with a broad mouth
broad-based with a narrow mouth
sized for cereal, soup, salad
cradled in open palms,
empty bowls

a trimmed base, light weight,
even walls, exterior etchings
all testify to the artist's skills
pock-marked, splotchy,
rough-edged, sooty-sided
open-mouthed, technique
or proletarian effort
empty bowls

containers stacked three deep
embraced by hungry buyers
tender turnings for final examination
signature incisions, deep cuts in warm clay
or tentative, shallow, scrapings in striated bases
other names flow in bold strokes
one-of-a-kind reminders
empty bowls

soup, bread, water
a simple picnic in a gravel garden
sun chases cold wind into shadows
children's chatter mingles with music
while elders dine in loose circles
all fill vacant spaces
barren places
empty bowls

Accommodations

Sometimes when he looks in the mirror
he sees a fractured Picasso,
all those lines and brittle angles,
those accommodations.

Up before dawn, he exercises
so he can bend to stroke the deaf dog,
to cue her when he walks to another room,
perhaps the kitchen,
or today he might leave the house,
change the air filter in his sister's
ceiling (she has balance issues),
shop for liquid soap or toilet paper
for his mother who can't remember
his name.

         Tomorrow
he'll fish with his grandson
who flew across five states
for a forty-six hour visit,
but he has to share the boy
with his ex-wife
who has a swimming pool and floats
filled with the passive aggressive
breath of her anger, so
he'll probably only get five hours.

Nothing ever quite fits.
He wonders if he can break apart
pieces of his life at the seams,
mosaic them into some kind of whole,
build a work of art from shards.

The Golem Moves to Cut-N-Shoot

Enough of that frigid attic,
Prague's brutal winters
that last hundreds of years.
No more fringed rabbis chanting
Cabalistic prayers for my creation,
demanding my protection against Blood
Libel, lies of the ignorant or evil
determined to pursue their own agendas.

A rabbi created me, left me voiceless,
cruel irony for one with EMET: Truth
etched across a clay forehead.
His G-d never breathed a soul into me,
yet he demanded my blind obedience,
called me a monster for my violence,
repented for his mis-conception, and
killed me by wiping out a single Hebrew letter.
EMET transformed to MET, my "death."
I was never loved.
Rage brought me back to life.
I escaped while Jews prayed;
Shabbat means nothing to the soulless.
I joined a security force,
exchanged my inhumanity for passage to Texas.
where I covered my tattoo with a cowboy hat,
joined the Aryan Brotherhood,
became one of many clay men with empty eyes
who believe truth lies in their tattoos.

Reverse

Texas girls dream
of good-looking blue-eyed
boys in pick-up trucks--
maroon Ford, burnt orange
Dodge, reflective white Chevy
for those super hot days.

Never one of those girls,
I dreamed of writers
or history professors
with enormous libraries
and houses full of art
conversation, laughter.

Such a strange twist
that now I'm bumping
and giggling in the backseat
of a green Avalanche
squeezed between twins, blue-
eyed boys in child safety seats.

An Articulate Arm

A darkened window opens,
and an arm emerges.
One manicured finger
indicates items on the menu--
down left, pause, upper right.
The dance steps continue.
Cars stack up behind.

The arm withdraws and
the car moves forward to a microphone,
where the draped limb extends again,
makes its lofty points.
At a response, the hand drops,
a presumption of the listener's ignorance.

The coach glides to a third stop
where the arm holds court,
issues royal decrees and a credit card.
Coffee appears, a cache of cream,
a bagged banquet, cupped
hands of mystery condiments.

Six feet from the drive-through
she pauses next to the garbage chute.
Fingers open over scorched pavement,
releasing crushed paper,
scraps of transparent wrappers
a final articulate statement of disdain.

#38046

Thirty years it hung above my fireplaces,
a Wyeth-stark landscape with a decaying barn,
one side naked, floors and loft open
to wind, rain, unforgiving sun.
At one side, a lean-to wobbles
on three uneven supports.
Starry wildflowers, pale blue,
sprinkle light over the April green rise.
Bare fence posts mark boundaries.

A prisoner created this, my first art
purchase, an original I could afford.
Money from sales bought inmates
cigarettes, Hershey bars, soap.
Numbers hidden like files on canvas
backs identified artists.
I wrote to my number.
He replied a few times, this thief,
told me his jailhouse friend painted it.
Rattled, he asked me not to write again,
                              and I obliged.

Now I see that barn,
        free as my Texas hill country,
        threatening to that fragile inmate,
        open to all he lacked.

Disarmed

Merry flags wave overhead at sunset,
as children drowse in shadowed corners,
moist heaps. Relieved of his stifling helmet,
and clanking armor, a knight limps
to the red and white striped pavilion,
lowers himself onto the bench, knotted
muscles and an oozing leg wound
reminders of his mortality.

With bruised fingers,
he summons the comely wench,
admires breasts barely restrained
beneath her kirtle as she bends over
with a flagon of mead and a sly glance
reserved for survivors of jousts,
winners who might enjoy a hearty tussle
of another kind, share pouches lined with gold.

She returns with crusted meat,
cakes sticky sweet with strawberries,
He pushes both away, waves
for another pitcher of ale
not yet drunk enough
to eat this leg of lamb, so like
his opponent's dismembered limb.

The Protector

An unexpected text.
Silent alarms sound.
A child is in trouble.

Within minutes
an undercover agent
in a navy jogging suit
and running shoes
peers from behind
a brick column.

When the sentry
at the front desk
turns to a ringing phone,
the agent slips in,
bypassing the ModCom
identification system,
and tiptoes down
hushed halls to an alcove.

Back to the wall,
the protector waits.
A break comes as
muffled footsteps
announce movement.
Children file out,
herded by guards with
lips set in thin lines.

A hush settles.
Mission on track.
The agent moves in,
spins the combination.
As the lock clicks open,
the agent's head snaps

right, then left,
before she places inside
a blank sealed envelope.

Hand over hand
to mute the mesh
of metallic locks,
the agent closes the locker,
steals her way to a pair
of doors at halls' end.
A rug caught
on the threshold
holds one ajar,
permitting
an alarm-free exit
into a car-filled lot.

Behind closed doors
a principal studies surveillance
screens, shakes her head,
and swings around in her chair.
"Mary," she says to her secretary,
"Mrs. Morris is on a mission again.
Little Mason forgot his homework."

Openings

Each time he returned home
to his family's cluttered flat
in blue collar New Jersey,
he opened a drawer in his wooden desk,
looking for something among the jumble
of pennies, pencils, postcards, protractors.
Each time she watched him, wondering
what he hoped to discover among
discarded pieces of his childhood.

In time, the desk traveled
to DC, then Atlanta, arriving
in Texas just in time for a new
generation to hide treasures.
Not once in decades of family life
did he examine the contents
of that drawer as he once had,
head tipped, eyes and fingers
lingering over each item.

Today the abandoned desk sits
alone, banished to a bare room.
From a wobbly frame
on the inlaid leather desktop,
his daughters smile from a photo,
hug each other's waists.
The center drawer holds
theatre tickets, invitations, postcard
reminders, none addressed to him.

She tugs on the brass handles,
stares at the open drawer's simple contents,
wonders what he once longed to find,
what missing pieces of himself.

Shuffling the Deck

An unseen hand left
a cache of poker chips
in the mailbox at the end
of her winding driveway.
The mailman wondered,
but the young mother with cancer
filled both hands with the bounty,
cried quiet tears, treasured
the gift, colored plastic disks
neighborhood babysitting currency,
mothers helping mothers swaddle
babies and each other with love.

Home Depot

She wanders
from behind a rattling
basket and tips her head,
then begins to dance.

Arms wide above her swishing
flowered skirt, she juts out her rear
end and bounces, feet stomping
to the rhythm, hands clapping
and swinging, open-palmed
to catch the next note.

Men, arms heavy with ball pein
hammers, painter's tape, wooden
baseboard trim, stop to stare.
Smiles turn up edges
of their lined lips
and they nod before moving on.

Maybe it's the round blue eyes
fringed with dark lashes,
or the wisps of curls
that frame her fair face, or
her open-mouthed delight.

Like this two-year-old,
they hear the piped in music
for the first time.

Scrappers

Dented pick-ups rattle
down suburban streets at dawn
after residents, with military precision,
wheel recycling bins and garbage cans,
drag roped bundles to the curb.

Sharp-eyed drivers
sniff air for carrion,
zoom in, pluck
a discarded traveler's trunk,
three-legged table, rolled rug.

But these aren't wreckers,
those foragers of the Cornish coast
who once lured ships onto rocks,
slashed survivors for plunder
washed ashore.

No, these scavengers
crate liquor, skim heated
pools, polish silver.
Quick-witted, they survive
on the excess of others.

Native Sons: Letter for my Brother

ekphrastic poem inspired by Natasha Trethewey's *Native Guard*

Our fathers' eyes, a steely gray,
not my skin, brown
like the earth I plowed,
gave me away.

Your mother never noticed my eyes,
I was only a houseboy, after all,
until you, in a fit of jealousy told her
you had seen me with Father in his study,
sharing books you were too lazy to read.

She banished my mother, the upstairs'
maid, lithe and lovely, to the fields,
where whipped by the winter wind,
burned by the summer sun,
she soon died.

When Father followed her in death,
then you, my brother, sold me.
Loss lodged in my empty heart,
a cold stone I carried as I read
the stars and fled north, away
from you, the white brother I despised.

So why now, as a Union soldier,
Native Guard ordered to write
this final letter to your loved ones,
do my tears fall across the page,
blurring ink, as I see you,
drenched in our shared blood,
our father's eyes, steely gray,
staring in death beyond my own.

Straightened Out

The only hints of my weakness:
a jutting neck, an occasional limp,
silvery scars slipping out from bare
necklines. Metal detectors herald
what lies beneath, two feet of titanium
bracing my garden-hose-twisted spine.
Doctors nod and smile at twin rods
glowing white in x-rays,
proud they wiped out a curse,
a wheelchair-bound destiny.

At times fiery fingers claw my hips.
On damp winter days, muscles
tighten over metal anchored to bone.
Doctors dismiss a painful cross
bisecting my spine beneath shoulder
blades, muscle knots at ends of rods,
expected, they say, in a bionic woman.

If they spent only one day
performing back-to-back
surgeries, standing inside
their masterpiece, my body,
that one day would wipe out
every smug smile,
every indifferent shrug.

III. Passages

Trains

I. Conroe, TX: 1959

At Union Station patent shoes
tap across the great expanse,
excite whirlwinds of dust as we emerge,
line up on the bench near the tracks.
Bump, bump. Bump, bump.
Impatient heels thump against wood.

A horn announces the train's
arrival from behind a brick building.
We jump up on the vibrating platform,
cheer as the rumbling engine appears,
slows, slides by, and stops.
Time for my birthday adventure.

A limping man places a box
beneath metal steps. We dance
past the weathered conductor,
scurry to facing seats,
wave out the window,
where Daddy, hat in hand, smiles.

I raise my eyebrows as the train lurches
forward, crosses the bayou,
clacks, "Go back, go back."
My sister and I count telephone poles.
One hundred poles from Houston,
and Mom says we're barely on our way.

Like a movie, scene after scene
flashes by, an enlarged version
of villages in my uncle's model train set:
box houses, bike-riding boys, barking dogs.

long wooden arms at railroad crossings,
where beetle-backed cars wait for us to pass.

Cows graze in open fields,
meander past rocking oil pumps.
Prairies give way to East Texas
piney woods. Lumberyards line
the tracks. Anticipation builds.
We're almost there. Conroe!

Stepping off the train, I smooth down
my plaid shirtwaist, rub my dusty shoe
against the sock on my other foot
and look up... at nothing,
only an intersection of tracks,
on a shell surfaced lot by a white shack.

Then I see my father, still smiling,
with a picnic basket, a Thermos
on the station wagon's open gate.
We lick melted chocolate from cookies,
gulp icy lemonade, and turn
freckled faces to the sun.

II. Mexico, DF: 1969

At Buenavista Station
I left him,
my first love,
his blue eyes rimmed
red as we kissed
again and again.

When the night train rocked
away, north to Texas,
I lay on a berth,
arms crossing my chest

stunned by the bands of loss
growing tauter with each mile.

Eighteen, I couldn't predict
future detours and destinations
so I wrapped crystalline
memories in tissue, layer
after layer, like a wedding gown
never worn.

I dozed
but my eyes opened
again and again
to flashes of cactus,
arms outstretched,
goodbyes to dimming stars
veiled in distilled light.

III. Night Train, Germany: 1990

Brandishing bottles, jostling,
pointing and laughing,
they arrived in second class,
their burly bodies pushed forward,
blocking our exit.

Guttural exclamations pressed
against us where we sat on a berth
talking about Grimm's fairy tales,
real castles, and a German grandmother,
long dead.

Age nine, my daughter, never silent, was.
I should have hissed like a mother cat,
but the stench of bodies and beer
permeated our small compartment,
consumed my breath.

My eyes darted between our captors
and my daughter, her sleek Dutch boy
bangs, creamy skin, and dimples.
But their eyes were on me.
I looked down.

At last they moved down the hall, bellowed
coarse words. My child tucked under one arm,
I held my breath until my husband arrived.
I bolted from the bunk and slid the door shut.
No latch.

Officials came. They demanded the surrender
of our passports for two borders crossing overnight:
Swiss-German and German-Dutch.
Standard procedure not to wake passengers
for documents.

My heart pounded.
I pulled ours from a duffel bag.
One hand pressed against
the silver filigree Star of David
tucked beneath my blouse.

The train jerked to a start.
A black man entered,
studied the compartment,
laid his suitcase beneath my bunk,
and retreated to the hall with my husband.

Long after the train rocked our daughter to sleep,
he and my husband returned to the unlit room .
I heard rustlings, saw nothing.
The train raged through the darkness
while we lay, stacked three deep,
Buchenwald somewhere outside.

At midnight the train stopped.
I listened as boots approached.
The door slid open.
I kept my eyes closed,
that childhood trick, that wish
for monsters not to find us.

Flashlight beams, whispered words
whirled around me.
They interrogated the black man
in hoarse bursts, even though
he had told my husband he was a German
resident and led him away.

I lay shivering, open-eyed,
blind to the rolling Rhine,
castles perched on mountain
ledges, pristine vistas.
My Germany was harsh
whispers, cold fear, black night.

IV. Niagara Fall Border: 2007

The train stops in a bare
field, devoid of color.
A solitary man in chinos
and a faded green polo
stands with hands in his pockets
scanning the train's lower half.

Uniformed men enter the train
from the other side
advise us that anyone without
a US passport must leave the train
to be interviewed in an unseen office.
Our instructions are clear:
no laptops, cell phones,
conversations, bathroom

breaks, trips to the dining car,
until everyone is cleared.

An old woman across the aisle
who cannot walk
and needed help finding
her glasses, her ticket
and her tin of tuna
tells them she is Jamaican
traveling alone between
her daughter in Toronto
and son in New York City.

The officials speak politely,
but take her from the train.
She disappears, carried
somewhere I can't see
from my side of the train.
I curse her children.

Outside our observer
paces the trains length,
peers beneath the carriage.
Routine inspection
or specific threat
out here in no-man's-land?

My calm frightens me,
relief that our government
protects us, that I,
a smug citizen, am safer.
When the inspectors
return the Jamaican,
they speak with the kind
condescension that comes
from strong young men.
USA! USA!

V. Houston's Herman Park Zoo: 2014

In a double stroller the boys
wait blank-faced as Smaug,
the six foot Komodo Dragon,
stretches out behind them.
They study the giraffe mama
lumbering across a dusty pen,
point to the elephant's trunk reaching
up to pull down straw from a feeder.
One twin, fearless, pats the goat
in the pungent petting pavilion,
trumpets his bravery
to his laid-back brother who,
ten feet away, warily watches.

On the zoo train wind ruffles
their thick hair, chestnut in winter.
One bounces on my lap, fingers silver
bolts on red metal seat frames,
laughs as he climbs the wooden
slats to reach his father on the other
side. The other, cheek-to-cheek
with his mother, chews on one
slippery finger, even as he chortles,
his smile so like hers, his blue eyes,
hers brown lit by each discovery.
Our unexpected joy boys
and I am here with them.

A Year in Haiku

Spring

yellow half-moon eye
scaly clouds, silver on black
alligator sky

                          tugging cockleburs
                          stuck in puppy's tangled fuzz
                          sunflower's last laugh

Summer

under cactus plants
armadillo bungalow
dugout hide-a-way

                          lick peach juice from lips
                          anticipate velvet touch
                          pit cracks bicuspid

Fall

cranberries simmer
cinnamon, sugar, orange
Thanksgiving delight

                          under gold street light
                          falling leaves spiral and twist
                          animated film

Winter

latticework aprons
adorn peeling ranch porches
wrinkled women wait

                          souls, all who loved me,
                          shroud me in pillowy arms,
                          honeyed memories

Rambler

Freedom came in a pink Rambler.
When my sister fled to college,
my parents gifted me a fifty dollar
car and a list of errands.

At fourteen, that first sweet taste
of independence came with an unspoken
promise, my own escape
just around the next bend.

California Dreaming: LA 1966

Dad made sales calls.
I gawked from tour bus windows,
screamed through amusement park rides,
snapped my Instamatic in movie studios.

Under fading skies, we dined
al fresco with his friends in Bel Air,
perched on wrought iron chairs,
my eyes averted from the naked
statue that peed water into the pool.
Their daughter, three years older than my fifteen,
had a fiancée, a graying movie executive.
We were a long way from Bellaire, Texas.

One night we cruised Sepulveda and Sunset,
scanned flashing signs. We stopped.
Dressed in a hot pink granny dress
I had struggled to sew on Mother's old
machine, which knotted thread, tight
as my adolescent emotions, I jumped out,
shaking the sleeves sewn in backwards,
But I tossed back my shiny straightened
hair, and smiled at our adventure,
our goal to get into Whiskey a Go Go.

Percussion and bass guitar throbbed from the doorway.
My heart raced as Dad shouted to someone in the shadows.
When he turned to me, creases lined his high forehead.
He shook his head. Neon flashed orange and green,
strobed across our faces. He studied me.
I shrugged. We threaded our way
through streets crowded with beaded hippies.
We'd do Disneyland together tomorrow.
Not much time left.

Murder

after Kevin Prufer's "Two Poems"

In 1970
    Halloween at a commune in rural Missouri,
university students sit in a circle
    pass joints
      and bottled beer.

    The wooden floor creaks as people
    shift their weight , squint in smoky
 haze and silence. I kill them all.
A wink terminates
    those who meet my sober eye.
        in a game called Murder.
I work the room with skill, the intoxicated
    disarmed under my sober gaze
      or impervious to my fleeting looks

           in other directions.

Nothing moves in the thick air, but the opening and closing
        of my lethal eye.
One by one they drop.
    My focus surpasses
  their torpor.
      I rejoice.

In 1988,
    I hang from my seatbelt,
      suspended sideways over a highway,
    my shuddering car now still
I turn my eyes toward the hiss,
    a crushed radiator,
      menacing chemical drip.

At last a man's face appears

above me
on the other side of the shattered glass.
He directs me to push open the door.

I struggle;
the door's weight defeats me.

Still he does not touch me.
He disappears
and I dangle
He returns, suggests
a route out
through tortured metal.

I let   myself
down,
crawl through the mangled frame
emerge through the hatch,
blinking in white-hot September sun.

In the blink of an eye, I see:
my flipped Volvo, clipped
coupons, lesson plans,
daughters' toys scattered
across five empty lanes.

Cold Catsup

tied tongue at face-to-face first meetings
egg with a pinprick crack in a sticky carton
winter gray rain dammed in gutter
needle on vinyl record
mud ridged on New Balance soles
mint green toothpaste at bottom of tube
F-key on out-of-tune piano
minute hand at 4:45 pm on Friday
baby's rubber duck in original packing
prehistoric Elmer's glue in nozzle
stuck, like me

New Year: 5764

Your indifference
renders me invisible
as I watch you
through the panes
in the French doors.

You thumb through
the book of love poems
you gave me
on my first birthday
spent with you.

Today,
thirty-four years later,
you study each page,
pursuing the perfect poem
to send to your new love.

It's not enough for you
to steal my dreams.
Now
you annihilate
my memories.

Bee Mine

His wife and daughters buzzed through his life like Queen Bees,
For fifty years he filled their Februaries with punny valentines,
Milk Duds, small stuffed toys, satin hearts, long witty letters.
His laughter was the putty that filled family fractures
even as his asbestos scarred lungs squeezed life from him.

One Valentine's Day, an ambulance brought him home,
his first night that year under his own roof.
His daughters tied heart-shaped balloons
at the foot of his metal-railed bed, their turn, they said,
when he grieved over not having presents for them.

Three days later, his daughters untied the lifeless balloons,
tossed them into trash bags, waited for removal of the hated bed.
They cursed their stupidity, wondered if with each labored breath,
he had watched the helium drift away as he drifted away, their gifts
Cupid's arrows, the sharpened corners of love and loss.

What I Miss

The bumping of shoulders
when sitting side-by-side
unspoken messages about things
seen or overheard.

Slow dancing, strong
shoulders or the back
of a neck beneath my fingertips,
my lips brushing prickly skin.

The smell of a man,
that earthy hint of sweat
beneath shampoo,
soap, aftershave.

Whole arguments
triggered or
squelched
with a single glance.

Fingers intertwined
Walking down the street
Hands held or toes touching
Reciting prayers side-by-side.

Weekend breakfasts
shared cantaloupe, bacon,
French toast, swapped
sections of newspaper.

Car rides
my mind in neutral
one hand on his thigh
miles of anticipation.

His laughter when he discovers
me wearing a pea green slicker,
pouring spaghetti sauce
over a mountain of tomato.

Fighting over who had the book
first, possession of the remote,
who should have said what
to which child.

Thirty-three years,
of shared history, memories.
I miss the intimacy, not the man,
who threw it all away.

My Dellight

Your glow summons me in the midnight dark house.
Come here, you whisper. I have something to show you.
I roll over, away from you, pull the covers up higher,
block your seductive light. But I just can't get enough--
your warm keys under my fingertips, your invitations
to shop, talk with friends, look up the latest stock
quotes, check on storms, or locate a lover, a Real Player.

You Excel at entertainment. My iPod downloads
your love songs or I dance Quick Time with YouTube.
My Explorer can no longer be left at home
so now you travel with me, by my side, or even in my lap.
I'm never without your PowerPoint, a charged battery,
flash drive. I won't allow anything to separate us,
even for a minute. I give you my Word.

Last Dance

I can still see you
dancing around
the living room
with our girls.
Willie Nelson crooned
from the stereo.

Their giggles spilled
like the thick curls
that tumbled down their backs.
They clung tightly to your neck,
heads tipped back in dizzy delight
as you two-stepped through the house.

I stood to the side,
laughing,
until you dropped
little ones on the couch
and pulled me out
to dance cheek-to-cheek.

But now our daughters
are poised young women,
soon to be lovely brides.
You will dance with them
cheek-to-cheek
at crowded receptions.

They will try to smile
for friends and family
as I stand to the side
knowing they wonder
if their husbands
will dance out of their lives
too.

Broken

She should have known it wouldn't be easy;
she never was good at making a clean break.
Those light bulbs for cathedral ceilings?
She stuck them on suction cups
at the ends of long poles,
but she never got one screwed in.
They tumbled back on her, splintering
all over the floor. She had to banish
the dog, sweep, and mop up slivers.
It would have been easier living in the dark.

So she should have known it wouldn't be easy
the day she picked up a bleeding marker,
listed her husband's betrayals
on the white porcelain plate
from the thrift shop, ten for a dollar.
She hurled it against a brick wall.
Nothing. Not even a chip marred its surface.

She launched the plate over and over,
smashed it against the concrete patio.
Finally it fractured like the marriage vows
she had honored for three decades.
She should have known it wouldn't be easy.
The revelation was that sweeping up
could feel so damn good.

House Finches

Birds, faded brown and dull gray,
fly between egg-shaped nests, sit
side-by-side, or roost on bare branches
in a glass case outside the dining room.
A slight woman stops each time she passes,
coos and chortles and smiles at the birds,
which never chirp back.
                        Someone leads
her to a table. She creeps along, at times
stopping to focus on something unseen.
At last she eases herself into a chair,
rests her birdlike arms on the table and waits
with the others for food.
                    No one talks, but
one gentleman holds out a plate of cornbread
muffins and another nods thanks or a greeting.
Wordless, their kindness sings.

Vertigo

Some people like spinning
                    the giddy rotation
  things randomly appearing,
                              disappearing from the periphery
a slow motion out-of-control
              inability to focus
                        tasted
      in tea cup rides
          wine glasses   tokes   pill bottles

    But close your eyes
                  for even a moment
  and the dizzy darkness
      sucks you in
                circling in-and-out
      a sickening spin
lifting yourself up

                        challenging as
                              climbing Himalayas

    The trick is to keep moving
                    run a hand along a brick wall
cling to the icy metal railing
                    teeter on the stained
      curb
              grab someone's arm

      until it passes
keep moving
                              no matter

          what

New Wheels

They have 3 wheelers and 4 wheelers
with front wheel drive,
says the one in the Astros cap.
He speaks in short bursts.
Mine turns on a dime,
steers like a dream,
even in reverse.

Uh-huh, nods the other
digging his fist into his pocket,
rattling his keys.
They huddle over hot red paint.

This baby has electromagnetic brakes;
Just switch off the power to stop.
Goes downhill--slow too.
See the turn signals
and dual LED headlights?

Would you believe this steering
wheel folds down? Battery's
over seven years old,
and has lifetime service.

So this what you do;
Find people like me,
pick their brains.
He taps his hat
Use what you want.

A white-haired woman
hobbles through an interior door
leaning on a four point cane.
Well, gotta' go.
The wife, you know.

I wish you success.
You'll love getting yours.

The cowboy waves his baseball cap
to listeners lining the faded walls
in a neurologist's chill waiting room,
throws his scooter into silent reverse
and guns it out the door.

Dessert

My floured fingers pressed
rolling waves into the crust.
With silvered tongs I cracked
each nut, picked out pieces, rejoiced
as they rose to the syrupy surface.

I gave my mother and her brother
bronzed perfection, pecan pie,
their favorite, my first,
and laughed as they argued
over who had the biggest piece.

Gripped by Alzheimer's
tightening fists,
now they can't remember
food names
or my name.

When I bring them together,
two souls whirling through the void,
there's a docking of walkers
for hugs and kisses,
no fights over store-bought pecan pie.

Now I want that first pie back--
every pearl of dough,
every meaty nut plucked
from splintered shell,
every oven-warmed sweet bite.

Vortex

the faucet drips hot, as time
slips by on a broken clock
steam clouds my mind
words lost in a swirl
metal handles mock
as hammered drops
chip away thoughts
that no longer stick
memories ripped
panic grips me
what is that
why can't I
remember!
how to
turn
it
off?

Departed

Driving down Buffalo Speedway
I caught a poem in my dream keeper,
titled it Jagged Edge,
but it vanished when I keyed in 1027,
code for the Alzheimer's unit
a number lost to Mom and Kay,
so much younger, my age.

Jagged Edge.
my frayed thoughts reach,
find shredded copy paper, blank.
Jack-o-Lantern teeth on the Day of the Dead,
serrated blades, sticky and stained,
tattered mourning ribbons
pinned to black lapels.

I squeeze Jagged Edge
in a tender, lined hand
watch my pricked palms drip.
Somewhere in DNA chains
secretive, silent,
a poem lingers
unwritten.

Primordial

For men maybe it's thumping
bass or revving engines,
V of geese overhead,
or voluptuous breasts
on any woman walking
toward them.

But for me it's that smell,
my lips to downy head,
or baby soft neck,
the infinite new that screams
my name and, in its absence,
twists the tourniquet.

Inscrutable

Under fluttering eyelids, this fresh
from-the-womb infant dreams.
Emotions flash across her face,
change in an instant. She frowns,
wrinkles her brow. Her tiny lips
quiver. A smile erases that.

Awake, baby meets great-grandma
with round eyes, wiggles, chortles.
Both inhabit smaller rooms, close eyes
when light and color and sound are too much.
Downy-haired, they coo back and forth,
their worlds others' riddles.

Joy Boys

Too tired to resist my snuggling,
he buries his face in my sweater.
But when his twin brother laughs,
I hear his bubbling response
rise from between my breasts;
their matched easy joy
softens my hardened shell.

Lullaby of the Cranes

Ride into the sunset
on the back of a crane.
Capture the dying gold rays.
Another sweet day flies.

Recline on downy wings,
spread wide to glide.
Bronze and orange skies fade
to pink, a sun-warmed comforter,
feathery soft, pulled up snug.

Fly through darkened skies,
rush of air a lullaby,
prelude to a gentle landing,
sleeping on a sandy shore.

Transparencies

Women wear age like camouflage
Heads no longer turn at our passing.

Men
women and children
look right past us.
To fight the fade,
some don red hats
and purple boas.
Others slash scarlet
across poofed lips,
freeze faces with botox.
In neon greens, harvest oranges,
no widow's weeds
or white hair for them.

Invisible, I see and hear more.